PROMETHEUS BOUND

PLAYS BY HOWARD RUBENSTEIN

Agamemnon
by Aeschylus, translated
Britannicus
by Jean Racine translated and adapted
Brothers All
The Defiant Soul
The Golem, Man of Earth
Prometheus Bound
by Aeschylus, adapted
Romance of the Western Chamber—A Musical
with Max Lee
Shiloh
Tony and Cleo
The Trojan Women
by Euripides, translated and adapted

BOOKS BY HOWARD RUBENSTEIN

According to James
Becoming Free
The Good Friday Prayer
Maccabee: An Epic in Free Verse
Photographs
Romance of the Western Chamber: English-Chinese Version for Children
Mandarin Translation by Li-Rong Lilly Cheng
Illustrated by Moch Fajar Shobaru

PROMETHEUS BOUND

A Play

Adapted by

HOWARD RUBENSTEIN

based on the play

Prometheus Bound of Aeschylus

and the epic poem *Origins of the Gods* of Hesiod

Granite Hills Press™

PROMETHEUS BOUND
A Play
Adapted by
HOWARD RUBENSTEIN

based on the play *Prometheus Bound* by Aeschylus
and the epic poem *Origins of the Gods* of Hesiod

Published by Granite Hills Press™ 2020
SAN 298-072X ISBN 978-1-929468-39-3
granitehillspress@yahoo.com

Cover by Howard Rubenstein, based on an internet illustration by an unknown artist

Printed in the United States of America

To Judy

CONTENTS

PREFACE

My version of *Prometheus Bound* is freely adapted from the play of the same name attributed to Aeschylus, and also from Hesiod's epic poem *Theogony* [*Origins of the Gods*], and also from other poets known and unknown who contributed to creating Greek mythology. My sources were the Greek texts and English translations in the Loeb Classical Library: H. Weir Smythe, *Aeschylus I* [containing *Prometheus Bound*], Harvard University Press, 1922, 1956, Cambridge, Massachusetts; Hugh G. Evelyn-White, *Hesiod, Homeric Hymns, Epic Cycle, Homerica* [containing Hesiod's *Theogony*], Harvard University Press, 1914, 2000, Cambridge, Massachusetts. I am greatly indebted to the commentary found in the Cambridge Greek and Latin Classics, *Aeschylus, Prometheus Bound*, edited by Mark Griffith, Cambridge University Press, 1983, Cambridge, England.

Scholars have not been able to precisely date *Prometheus Bound,* but most consider it among Aeschylus's later plays. Also scholars are not unanimous about whether Aeschylus was even the author of the play. Finally, they are undecided as to whether *Prometheus Bound* was part of a trilogy or stands alone as a single play. To discuss these issues is beyond the scope of this Preface. I refer those interested to Mark Griffith's scholarly work mentioned above. My version stands alone as a single play.

In addition to the problems just mentioned, the play (as well as Hesiod's poem) has many puzzles and discrepancies. Discrepancies or variations in the telling of a myth abound in ancient Greek literature, even tellings by the same author. Such problems are the province of scholars. However, an audience coming to see a play—whether in ancient Athens, or in today's London or New York—does not expect or want to struggle with puzzles and discrepancies, but to be stimulated by ideas and to be entertained. Therefore, I have taken the liberty of providing some solutions to the problems. Here is an example: Prometheus assures the Olympians victory over the Titans by means of a trick; but, surprisingly, neither Aeschylus nor any ancient writer described just what that trick was; so I invented one. Also I have eliminated certain passages that were confusing or meaningless or incomprehensible to a modern audience; similarly, I have expanded on other passages to clarify them. A translator may not take such liberties. But I have not made another translation, even if I thought I could improve on the existing ones.

Instead I have made an adaptation. Scholars may object to what I have done, but I did not write my adaptation only for them. I especially wrote it for an ordinary English-speaking theater-going audience with the aim of making *Prometheus Bound* accessible, meaningful, comprehensible, and, I hope, entertaining.

Howard Rubenstein
San Diego
September 22, 2019

P.S. This play was scheduled for production off-Broadway at The Tank NYC, 312 W. 36th St., NY, NY 10018, September 2020, produced by Meghan Finn and directed by Ran Xia. Production was postponed because of the COVID-19 coronavirus pandemic.

San Diego
July 4, 2020

CHARACTERS

NARRATOR.

PROMETHEUS (Pro-MEE-thee [as in *thing*, not as in *them*]-us), the Titan God of Potters. The Titans were of great size and strength—just how great is unknown; but consider that their parents were Earth and Sky, and that Atlas, a Titan and Prometheus's brother, bore the heavens on his shoulders. For the sake of our play, a tall and well-built actor will have to suffice.

Prometheus was the creator of Humanity, which he made out of clay (I remind you that he was the God of Potters), for which today, apart from scholars, he is hardly known. He was also the thief of Heavenly Fire, for which, even among non-scholars, he is well-known.

HEPHAESTUS (Huh-FESS-tus), the Olympian God of Fire and the Forge, the blacksmith to the Gods. The Olympians were of human proportions. Hephaestus is of average height, stocky, and muscular, and has a pronounced limp. He carries a tool kit containing a hammer, four large spikes, a long chain with a manacle at either end, and a short chain with a fetter at either end. He wears a black chiton (KYE-t'n) [Greek tunic] and a blacksmith's apron.

OKEANOS (Oh-KEE-ah-nuss), the Titan God of Fresh Water (Lakes, Rivers, Brooks, Streams, and Fountains). His dwelling place is the fresh water stream that encircles the ancient mythological Greek world. Okeanos is the father of the CHORUS of Water Nymphs. He is tall, well-proportioned, and middle-aged. He wears a blue chiton.

> Translators call this character "Ocean," but that is highly confusing because he is not the God of salt water, but of fresh water. To avoid this confusion, I kept the classical Greek spelling of his name. Poseidon, not a character in the play, is the God of Salt Water, more exactly the God of the Sea [the Mediterranean]. Aeschylus and his Greek contemporaries apparently were unaware of the oceans that today are well known.

IO (EYE-oh). A young Greek woman beloved by Zeus, and the only mortal in the play. She is lovely and graceful, even though she has cow horns on her temples; and she is a dancer. She wears a sheer white chiton.

HERMES (HER-meez), the Olympian God who is the Messenger of the Gods. He is short and lithe with small wings on his sandals, which enable him to fly. He wears a silver chiton.

CHORUS of Fresh Water Nymphs, daughters of OKEANOS and minor deities. They have human proportions, are pretty and graceful, and are dancers. They wear sheer green chitons.

* * * * * *

TIME: Eons ago, soon after the Olympian God Zeus, son of the Titan Cronus, overthrew Cronus and the Titan Gods, and became Ruler in Heaven.

SCENE: The summit of a towering cliff at the edge of an inlet of the sea in the remotest region of the earth. A boulder on the cliff dominates the scene.

PROLOGUE

NARRATOR: Good evening, and welcome to our production of *Prometheus Bound*. Today much of the western world believes that God created heaven and earth. But the ancient Greeks believed just the opposite—that heaven and earth created the Gods. The first generation of Gods were called the Titans, who were great in size and strength. The next generation of Gods were called the Olympians, who were of human size and strength.

The hero of our play, Prometheus, was a Titan God and, like the other Titans, was great in size and strength, but unlike them was clever and kind, creative and intelligent, and had the courage of his convictions. Prometheus was the God of Potters, and as master of his craft—making objects from clay—he created Humanity, something for which he is not well known. He alone of all the Gods loved his creation. Zeus, an Olympian God and the new Ruler of Heaven, considered mortals stupid and evil, and decided to annihilate them by withholding Fire from them, in which case they would freeze to death. Prometheus, in defiance of Zeus, stole a spark of Fire from the sun, hid it in a fennel stalk, which has the natural shape of a small-basket, and gave it to Humanity, thereby saving it from certain death. Because of

Prometheus's defiance of Zeus and theft of Fire, Zeus decided to severely punish Prometheus. Here is where our play begins.

(*Darkness*)

ACT ONE

The summit of a towering cliff at the edge of an inlet of the sea in the remotest region of the earth. A boulder on the cliff dominates the scene. It is a beautiful day with a blue and cloudless sky. PROMETHEUS *and* HEPHAESTUS *enter together. They look at the boulder and carefully examine it; then* PROMETHEUS *casually leans against the boulder.* HEPHAESTUS *sets down his tool bag.*

HEPHAESTUS: Prometheus, we have arrived
at the ends of the Earth,
a wilderness where no one ever comes.

PROMETHEUS: Hephaestus, I like to travel
to new places.

HEPHAESTUS: Prometheus, I must carry out
the orders of Zeus, our Heavenly Father,
and bind you with unbreakable chains
to this rock high on a cliff overlooking the sea.

PROMETHEUS: Well then, do it!
You must not disobey Zeus!

HEPHAESTUS: This is your punishment
for disobedience to him.
You stole a spark of Heavenly Fire

that belongs only to the Gods
and gave it to Humanity.

I am the God of Fire.
Fire is mine. You stole it.
That was a crime,
and you have to pay.

You are headstrong and willful.
Zeus hopes by this punishment,
you will promise to change your ways—
give up your championship of Humanity,
submit to the will of Zeus,
and never again be disobedient to him.

PROMETHEUS: I cannot make promises
I may not keep.

HEPHAESTUS: Perhaps this rock
(*Laying a hand on the rock*)
and these chains (*Laying a hand on the tool bag*)
will make you change your mind.
Prometheus, I don't really want to bind you,
but somehow I must find the courage to do so.

PROMETHEUS: Dear Hephaestus,
you made those chains on your forge
specifically to bind me, so who are you fooling?
Besides, it does not take courage to bind me.
It would take courage *not* to bind me!

HEPHAESTUS: That would not be wise,
for then I'd be in as much trouble as you!
Prometheus, you are the cleverest of the Gods—
but not the wisest.
Look what you've brought on yourself!

No more shall you know the company
of the humanity that you love.
No more shall you gaze on a beautiful face
or hear the sound of a sweet voice
or feel the touch of a warm hand
or see the shape and movement
of an attractive and graceful body.
No more shall you take delight in anything!
Instead, this is what's in store for you:

You will come to hate the day
with its scorching sun and unrelenting heat,
and long for the cool of evening
and the coming of the stars.

And when at last the night does fall,
you will hate its bitter chill,
and long for the warmth of the sun
to melt the morning frost.

Never shall you find satisfaction,
but only never-ending torment.
See what comes of your love of Humanity!

Once you were greatly admired
by the immortal Gods,
but you disobeyed Zeus
by giving mortals Fire
they had no right to have.

Now you will be bound to this rock,
never sleeping, knees hardly bending,
pouring out cries never ending
that no one will ever hear.

Zeus suddenly finds himself almighty,
and those with new power
are exceedingly harsh.

PROMETHEUS: Why do you speak on and on,
delaying your work?
Why do you show pity for me,
a God hateful to all the other Gods?

HEPHAESTUS: Prometheus, time was
when we were friends.

PROMETHEUS: Yes, and once
Zeus and I were friends, too.
It is because of that friendship
he is king of Heaven.

HEPHAESTUS: Can I ever forget
when Zeus was making assignments,
it was you who advised him
to make me God of Fire?

PROMETHEUS: But you feel betrayed,
Hephaestus, because I gave Fire to Humanity.
Tell the truth! You, too, are angry with me.
Moreover, you fear Zeus more than you love me.
So get on with your work!

HEPHAESTUS: O Fire that I used to love,
how I hate you now!
Let someone else be God of Fire!

PROMETHEUS: Every job has its dirty work,
and someone has to do it.
So, Hephaestus, chain me and bind me!
What if Zeus should see you shirking?

HEPHAESTUS: The chains are ready.

PROMETHEUS: Well, then drape them!
Clamp the manacles! Pound in the spikes!

(HEPHAESTUS *takes hold of the long chain with manacles. He clamps a manacle on one of* PROMETHEUS*'s wrists. Then he drapes the chain diagonally across* PROMETHEUS*'s chest, around his neck, back diagonally in the opposite* *direction across his chest, and clamps the other manacle on the other wrist. Then he takes a spike, positions it through the holes in the cuff of a manacle, and partially hammers the spike into the rock. Then he does the same with the other manacle.* (If this is difficult to understand, imagine a modern dress shirt with holes in the cuff for cuff links. In the case of our play, the cuffs are made of steel and the "cuff links" are spikes.) PROMETHEUS*'s arms are outstretched at about a 45 degree angle. During the binding process,* PROMETHEUS *does not struggle, but on the contrary cooperates, watching with interest.*)

PROMETHEUS: Strike the spikes harder!
Drive them all the way in! Leave nothing loose!
I've been known to wriggle out
of the tightest situations.

HEPHAESTUS: (*Driving the spikes home*)
There's no way you can escape from this.
For all your cleverness, Prometheus,
when compared with Zeus,
you're really rather stupid.
And yet, I cannot help feeling sorry for you.

PROMETHEUS: Get on with it!
You're talking too much and taking too long!
Watch out, Hephaestus, lest you end up
feeling sorry for yourself!

HEPHAESTUS: Don't give me orders!
Don't tell me how to do my work!

PROMETHEUS: All right,
no more orders from me.
Now bind and shackle my feet!

(HEPHAESTUS *takes hold of the short chain with a fetter at each end. He clamps a fetter on each ankle. Then he takes a spike, positions it through the link nearest a fetter, and thoroughly pounds the spike into the rock. He does the same with the remaining spike.* PROMETHEUS *is now completely bound. He is not suspended, but is fully weight-bearing.*)

HEPHAESTUS: Well, Prometheus,
now you are bound!

PROMETHEUS: I hope so,
for in Zeus you have a severe supervisor.

HEPHAESTUS: Well, my job is done,
so it's time for me to go.
But tell me, Prometheus, are people worth it?
I don't see any of them trying to help you.

PROMETHEUS: How could they help me,
even if they wanted to?

They are mortals
and the immortal Gods are their enemies.

HEPHAESTUS: How ironic
that *Prometheus* means *Foresight*
when you've shown no foresight here.
(*Shaking his head in puzzlement*)
Well, I must go.
Goodbye, Prometheus.

PROMETHEUS: Goodbye, Hephaestus.

(HEPHAESTUS *picks up his tool bag, looks at* PROMETHEUS *one last time, shakes his head, and limps away.*)

PROMETHEUS: (*After a long pause*)
Never to see a human creature again!
(*Crying out in agony*) Aiee!
O great Sky above!
O swift winged breezes! O running river waters!
O countless sparkling swells of the open sea!
How you must be laughing at me!
O Mother Earth beneath my feet!
O Sun above, who sees everything!
Behold how a God is tortured by Gods!

(*Sobbing*) Suffering, sooner or later,
pays a visit to everyone,
and when it comes has to be endured.

What's the use of struggling
against the inevitable?

(*Shouting*) O vast Universe!
Look upon Prometheus,
who stole Fire from Heaven
and gave it to Humanity!

(*Pause, to the audience in confidence*)
No doubt, you want to know how I did it,
so I'll tell you: I plucked a spark
from the Heavenly Fire,
and hid it within a fennel stalk,
at the place where it forms a little basket.
Neither Zeus, nor Hephaestus,
nor any of the Gods saw me do it.
But when they saw mortals with Fire,
they suspected me at once
of giving it to them.
Well, that was my crime,
and this is my punishment—
bound in chains beneath the open sky!

(*Suddenly startled by the sound of flapping wings*)

What is this sound of flapping wings?
Whatever it is has a fragrant scent.
(*Anxious*) Still, why has it come?

(*Sound of louder flapping of wings*)

I am afraid!

(CHORUS *of Water Nymphs, bare footed, slowly and gracefully flapping their arms and dancing, entering from all directions and coming to rest surrounding* PROMETHEUS)

CHORUS LEADER: Prometheus, don't be afraid.
We are the daughters of Okeanos.
We are the Water Nymphs,
and love and admire you so.

CHORUS: (*Each member of the* CHORUS *speaks singly except where otherwise indicated.*)

From our fresh water caves
we could hear banging,
hammering, and clanging of chains.

It was hard to persuade our father
to let us come and see what the noise was about.

We came so quickly
on a swift-running breeze,
we didn't even take time
to put our sandals on.

PROMETHEUS: Water Nymphs,
why have you come—

to gloat over my torment?

CHORUS LEADER: Oh, no, Prometheus!
We did not come to gloat.
We came to confirm our worst fears.
We fully expected to find a Titan
chained and bound,
but we did not expect that Titan to be you!
A new God reigns in Heaven
with new laws.
He conquered the former Gods, the Titans,
children of Earth and Sky,
and hurled them
into the darkest and deepest reaches of Hades—
into Tartarus—
and there had them bound with chains.

PROMETHEUS: Oh, that he had hurled
and bound me there, too!—
where no one could see me displayed so
shamefully—
like a child's toy high in the air,
a wind chime of lamentation.

CHORUS LEADER: Who is so heartless
as to delight in your misery?
Who does not feel your torment and pain?

CHORUS: (*Together*) No one—except Zeus!

CHORUS LEADER: He is exceedingly angry;
and once he has made up his mind,
there's no changing it—
unless another God robs him of his throne—
if that were even possible.

PROMETHEUS: It is possible!
I have a secret that tells of Zeus's downfall.
He would do anything to learn it,
but I shall never reveal it—
unless he sets me free
and atones for my pain.

CHORUS LEADER: You are brave, Prometheus,
and won't give up your love of Humanity
despite your suffering.
But I fear for you,
if you continue to speak of Zeus this way.
Is there no safe harbor
to which you can steer your ship
on this troubled sea
and bring an end to your voyage of sorrow?
Perhaps not. Zeus is harsh.

PROMETHEUS: Yes. Zeus is harsh—
but he does hold Justice in his hand.
So I would be happy
if the day should come
when his anger cools,
and he releases me,

and we are reconciled,
and once again become friends.

CHORUS: Tell us what you did
to make him punish you so.

PROMETHEUS: It is painful for me
to tell the story—
but just as painful to keep silent,
so I may as well tell it.

Ten years ago,
the Gods began to quarrel,
as to which one
should be Ruler in Heaven:
Cronus, the Titan and great in strength,
or Zeus, the Olympian and Cronus's son,
and great in intelligence.

What began as a quarrel
soon turned into a war—
the War of the Gods,
a war that lasted ten years!
The Titans believed the way to win
was through force, violence, and terror—
the only means they knew.

CHORUS LEADER: The Titans were so powerful,
what chance did the Olympians have
against them?

PROMETHEUS: I knew that victory would come
not through might alone,
but also through cleverness.
So I devised a plan
on how to capture the heavenly throne.

First, I took the plan to Cronus and the Titans,
but they refused to listen.
Now those who refuse to listen are stupid.
So I asked myself,
can anything good come from stupidity?
And although I myself am a Titan,
I decided to support the Olympians,
for they are intelligent.

Then I went to Zeus to tell him of my plan.
He listened.
I said that I had discovered
a wondrous and delicious drink
that gave the illusion of unlimited power
but in reality made the drinker ever weaker.
Once the Titans drank it,
the Olympians could easily conquer them.

CHORUS LEADER: What did Zeus
think of your plan?

PROMETHEUS: He liked it,
and asked me to set it in motion at once.

So I went to the Titans,
while they were still celebrating
their many victories over the Olympians
in this war that had been going on for ten years,
and brought them this drink.
Its wondrous effect soon entranced them,
and they felt endless joy and power,
which only made them ask for more.
And when they imagined
they had unconquerable power,
Cronus, the Titan Father, announced
that this was the moment to attack the Olympians.
And that is how the War of the Gods
came quickly to an end.

The Olympians were victorious,
capturing the Titans and hurling them
into Tartarus,
the darkest and deepest reaches of Hades,
located as far below the underworld
as Heaven is above Earth.
There Zeus had them bound in chains
as I am bound here,
and where they shall remain forever.

And that is how Zeus, son of Cronus,
became king of Heaven,
taking his own father's place.
You see, to win a war,
not only brute strength

but also clever strategy is required.
It was I, Prometheus,
who put Zeus upon the throne
through a trick! (*Pause*)
But see what it has gained for me!
It is a disease of tyrants
to trust their friends least of all.

CHORUS LEADER: But didn't Zeus reward you
for making him king of heaven?

PROMETHEUS: Yes. No sooner
was he sitting on the throne,
than he assigned to the Olympian Gods
their special privileges.
Even though I was a Titan,
because I was the God who helped him most,
he asked me what I wanted to be.
Because I loved to model clay,
I asked him to make me God of Potters,
and he did so, allowing me to roam free
about Heaven and Earth as I pleased.
And so, with nothing better to do,
I created Man, my beloved creature,
from clay.

But Zeus, finding Mankind stupid and wicked,
was determined to annihilate it,
and the other Gods sided with him.
I alone had the courage to oppose him.

What creator would not defend his creation?
But Zeus was determined
to have Mankind perish from the earth.

CHORUS LEADER: How was he
going to accomplish that?

PROMETHEUS: By withholding Fire from them,
and letting them freeze to death.
So I secretly stole Fire from Heaven
and gave it to them.

CHORUS LEADER: *You stole Heavenly Fire?*

PROMETHEUS: Yes, to save Humanity
from certain death.
And after I gave them Fire,
I gave them Blind Hope.

CHORUS LEADER: *Blind* Hope?

CHORUS: What kind of hope is that?

PROMETHEUS: The hope of never again
fearing death.

CHORUS LEADER: You mean
you promised them eternal life?
But immortality belongs to the Gods alone.
To give it to mortals, mere creatures of a day,

is to make them into Gods.

PROMETHEUS: Yes.
I did promise them eternal life,
and that promise was a mistake.
It sent Zeus into a rage,
and gave him yet another reason to punish me.

CHORUS LEADER: Did you promise immortality
on condition that mortals worship you?

PROMETHEUS: No!
My love for Humanity is unconditional.

CHORUS LEADER: But I still do not understand
Why you promised it.

PROMETHEUS: I felt sorry for them,
and I wanted to comfort them.
Without Fire they knew they were
going to be annihilated,
so they were overwhelmed with fear.
Blind Hope took all dread away.
But it was wrong of me to promise that.
The gift I should have given
was to live comfortably
with Uncertainty and Doubt.

CHORUS LEADER: Well,
you did give them Life and Fire—

both great gifts.
And for the gift of Fire
Zeus punishes you with terrible torture.
Is there no end to it?

PROMETHEUS: Not unless
he brings it to an end.

CHORUS LEADER: Well, then, Prometheus,
admit your mistake,
and beg him for deliverance.

PROMETHEUS: The fortunate
are always ready to give advice
to the unfortunate.
But I shall never beg for my deliverance.
Still, I appreciate that you so earnestly
want to help me.

CHORUS LEADER: We are related.
Our father is a Titan like you.
So of course we pity you.

PROMETHEUS: (*Intimately*) Don't pity me.
Come, sit down here, closer to me,
and learn the fate that still awaits me.

CHORUS LEADER: Water Nymphs,
sit down by Prometheus
and listen to the rest of his story of woe.

(CHORUS *sits down around* PROMETHEUS.
OKEANOS *enters flying, and comes to rest
at the edge of the cliff.*)

OKEANOS: Hail, Prometheus!
I see that my daughters
have already arrived. Hello, girls!

CHORUS: (*Together*) Hello, Father!

PROMETHEUS: Hail, Okeanos!
Why have you come?
To accuse me of foolishness
in words of righteous indignation?

OKEANOS: I see before me a fellow Titan,
for whom I have compassion,
and not only because we are related by blood.
There is no God for whom I have greater respect,
for you are caring above all others!
Tell me how to help you
because in me you know you have a loyal friend.

PROMETHEUS: (*Crying out*) Look at me,
Okeanos!
Prometheus—a God, and once a friend of Zeus,
now tormented and tortured by him!
Have you come to stare at me
and pity me, adding to my misery?

What a sight! The friend of Zeus
who helped him gain his throne!
And this is his reward!

OKEANOS: I see my friend Prometheus.
So let me give you some friendly advice:
First and above all, know yourself!
Next, adapt to changes in circumstance!

PROMETHEUS: What are you saying?
That I should never have created Man?
But having created him,
I should have stood by
and watched him freeze to death—
not stolen Fire to save him?

OKEANOS: What I'm trying to say is this:
There is a new king in Heaven—Zeus.
And although on a high throne distant from us,
he is never far away,
and he may overhear you.
If you continue to provoke him
with harsh words from a sharp tongue,
your present sorrows will seem like child's play.
Zeus is a severe ruler
and accountable to no one.

PROMETHEUS: Okeanos,
do you have any good advice,
or do you just intend to babble on and on?

OKEANOS: Let me come to the point.
Cease your disobedience of Zeus
and reconcile with him, and your suffering will end.
You've never learned
when you've had enough,
but are always eager to take on more.
Give up! Admit that Zeus has won!
Prometheus, do you really think
you can change the world and make it right?

Listen to me: This is what I intend to do.
I will go to Zeus and plead your case.
After all, you are no ordinary God.
In the meantime, I ask only one thing of you:
Keep your mouth shut!
With all your intelligence,
you've foolishly never learned
what happens to someone
who only speaks the truth!

PROMETHEUS: Okeanos, fellow Titan,
I thank you for your friendship
and all you are trying to do for me.
So far you've said nothing to offend Zeus.
I want you to leave before you do.
You will be fortunate if Zeus does not punish you
for coming to visit me.
Please do not go to Zeus to plead for me!
He's not easy to persuade.

Say nothing on my behalf.
For if you do,
you'll only bring disaster on yourself.

OKEANOS: When anger reaches a fever pitch,
wise words can act like medicine,
and the fever will break.

Prometheus, you know how to give advice,
but you don't know how to take it!
You always think of others before yourself.
I owe my very freedom to you
because you reminded Zeus,
that even though I was a Titan,
I supported him, an Olympian,
during the War of the Gods.
So don't try to stop me from going to Zeus,
for I am confident that my speaking to him
will set you free.

PROMETHEUS: (*Annoyed*) Don't do it!
You certainly are courageous,
but your caring for me won't help me,
and will only harm you.

Surely you've heard
what happened to my brother, Atlas.
He sided with the Titans against Zeus.
But Zeus did not punish him,
as he did the other Titans,

by binding him with chains in Tartarus.
Zeus punished Atlas
by having him bear forever
the sky upon his shoulders—
not an easy thing to do—
on the West coast of Earth,
where Night and Day
greet one another as they pass,
one going up, the other going down.

What if Zeus does something like that to you?
Besides, if you speak up for me,
Zeus will think you're a fool.

OKEANOS: Sometimes appearing foolish
is the greatest form of cunning.

PROMETHEUS: (*Laughing*)
If Zeus suspects cunning,
he'll think I'm behind it,
and then you'll surely be severely punished!

OKEANOS: I don't think so.
Besides, you surely know
speaking the words
that are on your mind
can cure the insanity
of swelling anger
that leads to violence.

PROMETHEUS: Provided
one treats the soul in time.
Too much time has passed.

OKEANOS: But what harm can come
of trying?

PROMETHEUS: It's too late.

OKEANOS: Well, I can see
there's no point in talking further.
So I may as well return home.

PROMETHEUS: Yes, Okeanos,
go home. That's best.

OKEANOS: Farewell, Prometheus!
Goodbye, children!

PROMETHEUS: Farewell, Okeanos!
I appreciate your concern for me,
I really do!

CHORUS: (*Together*) Goodbye, Father!

(OKEANOS *flies off, waving as he goes.*)

CHORUS LEADER: O Prometheus,
the whole Earth—Europe, Asia, Africa,
and even the unknown continents—

laments for you!

CHORUS: The lakes and rivers weep.

The sea cries out
as the waters splash
and dash
and crash against the cliffs,
and the waves fall upon the shore.

(*Together*) All nature cries out
for their love of you.

PROMETHEUS: Water nymphs,
do not think I am ungrateful
to those who show affection for me.
But the truth of the matter is
I have no one to blame but myself.
You will understand that
when I tell you the whole story,
and the consequences
of my theft of Fire.

Yes. Fire saved Humanity from certain death,
but it did a great deal more.
Until I gave mortals Fire,
they had neither intelligence nor feelings.
They wandered about aimlessly,
living in caves
or like ants in tunnels beneath the earth.

So I breathed Heavenly Fire into them.
Fire illuminated their minds,
and suddenly they could think!
Fire inflamed their souls,
and suddenly they could feel!

Then I taught them how to use Fire
not only to keep themselves warm,
but also to cook their food
and light up their dwellings
and with torches to have nighttime celebrations.

With Fire I taught them
how to make pottery from clay—
an occupation that gave me the greatest delight—
and how to forge tools from molten metal.

I taught them how to read the stars
and how to recognize the seasons.

I taught them numbers,
which I invented for them,
the greatest of intellectual achievements.

I invented the alphabet—
and taught them to group letters into words
and words into sentences,
which enabled them not to depend on memory,
so fleeting and unreliable,

but to write things down, to keep records,
a permanent memory for future generations.
Now they could write history,
and compose songs and poetry.

I showed them how to domesticate animals—
to bring beasts of burden under the yoke
to relieve their hardest labors,
and to harness horses and ride them,
and drive chariots.

I taught them carpentry,
and invented boats and sailing ships.

I taught them to mine copper, iron, silver and gold,
treasures hidden within the Earth.
And I taught them how to make bronze.

I taught them the arts—
painting and sculpture and architecture.

How many are the wonders I devised for them,
but I can't devise a single thing
to bring my own suffering to an end!

CHORUS LEADER: Prometheus,
how good you've been to Humanity,
but you went astray when you disobeyed Zeus.

PROMETHEUS: You are too quick to blame!

Listen to the whole story,
and then judge me, if you will.

To heal the sick, I taught men
the art of medicine.
I gave them herbs and ointments
to take away pain.
I taught them how to set broken bones
and how to use the knife and cautery.
I taught them the basic principle
on which all medicine rests—
to show the sick you care for them.
That principle will always be essential,
even after the coming
of the greatest discoveries.
It was I, Prometheus,
who taught these things,
even though the God Apollo
and his son Aesculapius
will take all the credit.

I know you think I'm boasting.
Well, I am! I'm proud of all I've done for Humanity.
Because of my gift of Fire,
I lifted mortals up from savagery,
and set them on the road to civilization.

CHORUS LEADER: Prometheus,
surely there is a dark side to Humanity
your gift of Fire could not illuminate.

PROMETHEUS: Yes.
Before I gave men Fire,
they'd already acquired bad habits and customs.
So, yes, Mankind has a dark side
no Fire can brighten.

CHORUS LEADER: Tell us!

PROMETHEUS: They will observe a coincidence
and endow it with significance.
thereby giving meaning to the meaningless—
bird omens, animal sacrifice, human sacrifice, too.
I could not persuade them
to give up those superstitions,
for they had already cloaked them
in sanctimonious terms—
"ritual," "tradition," and "religion."
And the slightest differences in religion
gave different groups excuses . . .

CHORUS LEADER: To make up lies,
and call it Truth!

CHORUS: To disrespect one another!

To be cruel to one another!

To curse and hate one another!

To kill one another!

(*Together*) And to do all those things
in the name of Love!

CHORUS LEADER: Stop it! Enough!
Let's change the subject!

PROMETHEUS: What?! "Change the subject"?
You can't take it anymore?

CHORUS LEADER: Prometheus,
for your gift of Fire,
Humanity shall worship you one day
above all the other Gods.

PROMETHEUS: No, Destiny does not have that
in store for me.
The most I can expect
is to become the God of Potters.

CHORUS LEADER: What?! *God of Potters?!*

PROMETHEUS: Yes. Shaping clay
is what I loved to do most.
I made pots from clay,
and I made the first people from clay.

CHORUS LEADER: All the more reason
that people should worship you.

PROMETHEUS: No.
A God worthy of being a God
does not need or want Man's worship.

CHORUS LEADER: And yet,
mortals continue to make sacrifices to the Gods.

PROMETHEUS: Yes, but thanks to me,
they offer the worst parts—
the bones, the fat, the offal—
to the Gods, and keep the best parts—
the delicious meats—for themselves.

CHORUS LEADER: You can be sure,
Prometheus,
that Zeus also hates you for that!
Prometheus, tell us,
are you weaker than Destiny?

PROMETHEUS: Everyone is weaker than
Destiny.

CHORUS LEADER: Even Zeus?

PROMETHEUS: Even Zeus.
He cannot escape it.

CHORUS LEADER: Well, what is
destined for Zeus—

except to rule forever?

PROMETHEUS: His destiny is my secret.
When he sets me free, I shall reveal it.

CHORUS LEADER: May I never
be in conflict with God.

CHORUS: May I never offend a God.
May I always keep this vow,
and may it never depart like melting snow.

Oh, it is sweet to spend a life of happiness
with family and friends
celebrating joyous festivals.

I tremble, Prometheus,
when I look at you, racked by endless torture.

PROMETHEUS: My friends,
Affliction constantly roams the Earth,
and sooner or later visits everyone.

CHORUS: Prometheus, you have no fear of Zeus,
and you love Humanity too much.

Zeus was determined to destroy Humanity,
but you were determined to save it.

What good did you get out of helping

those creatures of a day?
What did they ever do for you?

(*Together*) Prometheus, Thief of Fire,
Savior of Humanity!

CHORUS LEADER: Prometheus,
do you really know what Mortals are like?

CHORUS: They know little,
so they think they know everything!

They are weak,
so they enjoy lording over others!

They are greedy, never satisfied,
always wanting more—
and they don't care how they get it!

They are insignificant,
so they want to be Gods!

CHORUS LEADER: Today they forge metal—
to make hoes and spades and plows
to cultivate the earth.
Tomorrow they forge metal—
to make swords and spears and arrowheads
to slaughter one another!

CHORUS: (*Together*) Prometheus,

Thief of Fire, Savior of Humanity.

(PROMETHEUS *cries out in agony, as darkness descends.*)

ACT TWO

The same scene, many years later. It is a beautiful night with a starry sky and a nearly horizontal crescent moon. The CHORUS *is lying about unobtrusively.* PROMETHEUS, *his head moving slowly from side to side, is scanning the sky. After awhile,* IO *enters, dancing in leaps and bounds, in a state of frenzy, accompanied in contrast by a lullaby, which is played on an oboe.*

IO: (*Abruptly stopping her dance, then gazing over the cliff*)
Where in the world am I? Where are the people?

(*She turns and is startled to see* PROMETHEUS. *She gazes at him for a long moment.*)

Who is this large creature bound to a rock?
He is so handsome!
What has he done to deserve such punishment?

(*Suddenly angrily swatting her arm*) Ouch!
I am constantly bitten by a horsefly,
and forever followed and hounded
by a giant cowboy in the sky.
The cowboy has a thousand eyes;
and while many of his eyes are asleep,
some of them are always awake, watching me
as I wander in my misery

over the rocky shores and sandy beaches,
hardly taking time to eat or drink,
never bathing in the sea.
All the while I am running and leaping frantically,
the cowboy plays a lullaby on his pipe,
trying to make me fall asleep,
while the horsefly that always bites me
makes sure I stay awake.
(*Swatting*) Ouch!

(*Gazing at Heaven*) O Zeus,
was my offense against you so terrible
that you punish me with constant torment?
Must I wander forever, be bitten forever?
Isn't there a God somewhere
who hears the cries of a young virgin
who is partially transformed into a cow?

PROMETHEUS: Io, I hear you!
And I've heard of you, too. You are famous!
(*Contemplating*) Io, your cow horns
cannot take away your beauty.
You are as lovely as the crescent moon!
Look! You are the very image of it!

(ALL *look at the moon.*)

No wonder the cowboy in the sky
cannot take his eyes off of you!

CHORUS LEADER: He is always staring at you.

CHORUS: Watching you.

(*Whispering, decrescendo*) Looking at you.

Looking.

Looking.

Looking.

Watching.

Watching.

Watching.

Staring.

Staring.

Staring.

PROMETHEUS: Io, you are so beautiful.
No wonder you set the heart of Zeus on fire
and filled him with desire.
But you denied him,
and so he is punishing you.
And his wife, Hera, is jealous,

and she is punishing you, too.
She sends the horsefly with the stinging bite
to torment you.
And so you are always running, jumping, leaping
wandering forever, frantically,
always yearning to rest;
and the cowboy's lullaby
makes your yearning for sleep even stronger,
while the horsefly's bite,
makes sleep impossible.

IO: (*Amazed*) How do you know all this?
And who are these lovely maidens?
And who are *you*, great one?
Speak to me, the wandering virgin of sorrows!

PROMETHEUS: I am Prometheus.

IO: O Prometheus! Great Titan God!
Creator of Humanity!
Mortal that I am, I owe my very existence to you!

What have you done to suffer so?
Is it possible that you suffer
as much as I? (*Crying out in agony*) Aiee!

PROMETHEUS: Yes, it is possible!
But I no longer cry out.
With the passage of time,
I've grown used to my torment.

IO: O great God, teach me to do the same!
But tell me, who bound you to this rock?

PROMETHEUS: Zeus willed it,
and Hephaestus did it.
By day I face the scorching sun,
by night the icy wind.
I endlessly yearn for death,
but death for me is impossible,
for I am an immortal God.

IO: O Prometheus, tell me,
what was your crime?

PROMETHEUS: I stole a spark
of the Fire of Heaven
and gave it to Humanity.

IO: *So! It was you who gave Humanity Fire?!*
You are the savior of Humanity!
And for that you are being punished?!

But tell me of my fate.
Will my suffering never end?

CHORUS LEADER: Io,
before Prometheus answers you,
tell us more of your story of torment!

IO: I am ashamed to tell it—
ashamed to speak
of the wild disturbance in my mind,
and how I developed the horns of a cow.
(*Reflecting*) But I feel I'm among friends,
so I'll tell you.

Once I lived a happy life
on my father's farm in Greece.
Then one night a recurring dream began.
That was the start of my troubles.
I saw strange apparitions sent by Zeus.
They smiled at me and whispered these words:

"Hail, Maiden, blessed by good fortune!
Why do you insist on remaining a virgin
when you—a mere mortal—
have the extraordinary opportunity
to make love with the greatest God of all?
Zeus is filled with desire for you.
Do not thwart his advances.

"Go to the meadow
where your father's cattle graze,
and there yield to Zeus and satisfy his passion.
And you will discover how much you enjoy it.
To disguise himself from Hera, his jealous wife,
Zeus will come to you in the form of a bull;
and in order for you to receive him,
he'll transform you into a cow."

CHORUS LEADER: Poor girl!
Those are indeed strange dreams!

IO: Finally I gained the courage
to tell my father of my dreams.
He went to Zeus's oracle at Dodona
to find out their meaning.
Each time he went,
he received ambiguous answers,
until one day the oracle spoke words
as clear as they were cruel.
My father was to drive me from his farm
and from my homeland.
I was to be an exile,
wandering the Earth.
Should my father disobey,
Zeus threatened to hurl flaming thunderbolts
at our town
and destroy it along with the people.
What was my father to do?
Against his will, and weeping inconsolably,
he sent me forth and banished me forever.
And all the joys of childhood
ended in bitter grief.

CHORUS LEADER: What a terrible thing
for a father to be forced to do.

IO: No sooner had I begun to wander

than I began to lose my mind
and change my shape.
Cow horns sprouted from my temples,
and a horsefly began to sting and bite me.
(*Swatting angrily*) Ouch!—
And so I began to run and leap in panic,
while in the sky,
the giant cowboy who never sleeps
fixed his myriad eyes upon me,
and began to play a lullaby on his pipe,
a tune to make me yearn for sleep,
while the horsefly's bite kept me awake!
(*Swatting*) Ouch!

Now you've heard my tale of woe;
and so, Prometheus,
tell me what's yet in store for me.
And do not hide the truth,
for blind hope given out of pity
is the worst affliction of all.

CHORUS LEADER: Zeus did this
because you refused to make love to him.

CHORUS: Are all men forever to punish women
who refuse to surrender to them?

CHORUS LEADER: And Hera, Zeus's wife,
torments you because Zeus fell in love with you.

CHORUS: Are all wives to punish women
whom their husbands fall in love with?

CHORUS LEADER: Io, in Zeus
you have an unsatisfied lover,
and in Hera you have a jealous wife.
That is a bad combination
and bound to end in misery.

PROMETHEUS: Io, when you leave
this remote and isolated land,
take the northern road
where the fierce and freezing north wind blows.

Soon a new road will appear
which turns east where the sun rises.
Follow the eastern road
along the rugged coast
until you come to the River of Violence,
which lives up to its name.
Do not ford that mighty torrent
but follow its banks until you come
to the Caucasus mountains,
whose peaks reach up and touch the stars.

There the River becomes a waterfall,
and there, too, is a mountain pass.
Take the pass. It turns south
to a land inhabited by women
who loathe all men.

Because you are beautiful,
they will treat you well,
and lead you to the Cimmerian isthmus,
which terrorizes sailors,
for there the sea opens ravenous jaws
that devour ships.

You will then come to the Maeotic strait.
Take courage and ford it.
Forever after,
Humanity shall speak of your crossing,
and in your honor
name that place “the Bosporus,”
which means “the place where the cow crossed.”
The Bosporus separates Europe from Asia.

Well, Io, haven’t you heard enough?
Zeus, our relentless tyrant king,
certainly has been torturing you
in your wanderings,
and what I’ve told so far
is only the beginning.

IO: Oh, oh, dear me! Dear me, oh, oh!
How can I bear it?

PROMETHEUS: *How can you bear it?*
What will you say when you hear
of the troubles yet to come?

IO: In that case, why go on living?
What is the purpose?
Why not end it here and now,
jump off this cliff into the abyss
and bring an end to all my suffering?
It is better to die all at once
than to linger and die little by little!

PROMETHEUS: No, not so! Look at me!
Death for me is impossible,
for I am a God and can never die.
There is no limit to the torture
Zeus can inflict on me—
unless he is removed from his throne
and hurled from Heaven!

IO: Zeus hurled from Heaven?
Who could do that?

PROMETHEUS: It sounds as if
that would make you happy.

IO: Why wouldn't it make me happy,
when he tortures me so?

PROMETHEUS: Then know this:
It is certain to happen!

IO: But who could do that?

PROMETHEUS: Zeus himself!

IO: Ah, that is a riddle.

PROMETHEUS: No, no riddle.
Zeus will make love to a certain woman,
and that will be his undoing.

IO: Is this woman mortal like me
or an immortal Goddess?

PROMETHEUS: Less than a Goddess,
more than a mortal.
And she shall bear a son greater than his father.

IO: A son greater than Zeus?
Who is this woman? And who is her son?

PROMETHEUS: I will not say. It is my secret
unless Zeus unbinds me and sets me free.

CHORUS LEADER: If you're not going
to reveal your secret, Prometheus,
then you may as well tell Io
of her future wanderings,
and who will set *her* free.

PROMETHEUS: Io,
when you cross the Bosporus
from Europe into Asia,

you will come to the great plains
where dwell three old-maid sisters
who look like swans,
majestic and beautiful birds.
Do not be deceived,
for if you observe them carefully
you will see
that these *beauties* share one eye
and one tooth between them.
Close by live their three sisters,
the Gorgons, who have wings of bats,
and squirming snakes for hair.
The gorgons are old hags and virgins,
so ugly even the sun and the moon
cannot bear to look down on them.
And any mortal who looks at them
will turn to stone and die.
So do not even glance at them
through the corner of your eye!
They are guardians of that land,
and the eldest sister,
whose name is Medusa, is their ruler.
Beware!

Next you will come to a stream
laden with gold,
which could make you very rich.
Do not be tempted to gather treasure.
Have nothing to do with it
nor with any of the monsters I've mentioned,

but run from that land as quickly as you can,
for everything and everyone you encounter
means to inflict harm upon you!

Head west, toward the setting sun,
and you will come to the African continent
and its dark people
who live along the Ethiopian River.
Follow its banks
until it pours out a great waterfall,
which is the source of the River Nile.

Follow the Nile to its delta,
where at last you will find rest,
and your journey will be almost over.

If there's anything you've not understood,
tell me now, Io, and I shall explain;
for I have more time to spare
than I know what to do with.

IO: I have nothing to ask,
for you've been perfectly clear.

CHORUS LEADER: Prometheus,
speak to us of Io's earlier wanderings.
For if she sees you tell the truth about her past,
she'll know you're telling the truth
about her future.

PROMETHEUS: Io,
when you left your father's farm,
you went to Dodona, where the oracle of Zeus
with its marvelous talking oak trees
spoke of your surrendering one day to Zeus.

IO: That is so.

PROMETHEUS: From Dodona,
you ran to the shores of the Sea,
and entered and crossed it.
Forever after, that part of the Mediterranean
will be called the Ionian Sea
in your honor,
and those who sail it will always think of you.
Now, Io, you know I speak the truth.

IO: Yes, you need not go on about my past.
Tell me more about my future!

PROMETHEUS: At the delta of the Nile,
Zeus will come to you,
this time not in the shape of a bull,
but in the form of a handsome young man,
a disguise that will fool even his wife.
And with a gentle touch, by the stroking
of your hair and your brow and your temples,
Zeus will restore your mind and melt your horns;
and you will once again become
a sensible and beautiful girl.

And God will make gentle love to you
that will fill you with pleasure.
Afterward you will fall into a deep sleep;
and when you awaken, refreshed and restored,
the horsefly pest that tortures you
will have flown away;
and the cowboy in the sky
will have ceased singing his lullaby
and watching you;
and his thousand eyes
will have become brilliant stars in the sky.

Then you shall sail from Egypt to Greece,
and return to your father's farm.
And when your time is fulfilled,
you shall bear a son,
your child with Zeus,
and shall name him "Caress"
because it was through caressing
that Zeus restored you to your former self,
and through gentle love-making
that you conceived your child.

And one day when your son matures,
he will marry
and have many children.
And your posterity,
descendants of Zeus and you,
will be great kings and heroes of Greece.

IO: So, I am not the woman
whose son is destined
to bring about Zeus's overthrow
and become the new God of Heaven?

PROMETHEUS: No. That is not your destiny.
That much I can tell you,
but the rest must remain my secret.
Let me remind you that Zeus falls in love
with many beautiful women—
you are not the only one!—
and he has yet to find the woman
who will bear the son
who will bring about his overthrow.

IO: Ah, me! All my wretched wanderings
with nothing to show for it,
and I shall end up where I started!
It's enough to drive me to madness once more!

PROMETHEUS: What?!
"Nothing to show for it"?
Do you think a posterity of heroes and kings
counts for nothing?

IO: Well, being the mother of heroes and kings
is not the same as being the mother of a God!
Why it is enough to make a girl mad!
(*Crying out*) Aiee!
No sooner do I mention madness

than it comes upon me.
And the horsefly pest returns to bite me—
(*Swatting angrily*) ouch!—and I am carried away
like a ship lashed by a storm.

My mind no longer understands
the words my tongue speaks,
and my thoughts tumble over one another
like a drowning man
tossed in tall and turbulent waves.

(*She exits as she entered, dancing and leaping frantically, to the tune of a lullaby, and swatting the horsefly.*)

CHORUS LEADER: It is best for likes
to fall in love with likes.

CHORUS: Should a poor boy marry a rich girl?

Should a commoner marry a king?

Should a mortal marry an immortal God?

Oh, may no God fall in love with me—
source of endless misery!

PROMETHEUS: Let Zeus go on believing
that lightning and thunder give him his power!
His son by the woman I know

will bring about his overthrow.

CHORUS LEADER: Till then,
he may still inflict punishment on you,
even harsher than you're receiving.

PROMETHEUS: Let him! I am prepared for it!

CHORUS LEADER: Prometheus,
show some humility!

PROMETHEUS: What you mean is
worship the God of the day!
Adore him! Kiss his feet!
And let tyranny triumph!
As for me, Zeus counts for nothing—
less than nothing!
Let him show his power, impose his will!
His reign will not continue much longer!

(HERMES *enters, flying. The* CHORUS *backs away, giving him room to land.*)

But what have we here?
None other than Hermes, Zeus's messenger boy!
He comes with good news, no doubt.

HERMES: Prometheus,
schemer, smart, and clever—
and bitter beyond all measure!

You have disobeyed Zeus,
and have betrayed the God of Fire,
all for the sake of mortals,
mere creatures of a day!
Prometheus, Thief of Fire!
(*Emphatically*) I am speaking to you!

PROMETHEUS: (*Politely*) And I am listening.

HERMES: Zeus is fully aware
that you know of a mortal woman
who will bear a son who will overthrow him.
He commands you to name that woman
and her son, the new God to come.
State the names clearly,
not in the ambiguous words of oracles!

PROMETHEUS: Hermes, how brave you are,
as becomes the darling of the Gods!
Well, you are young, and your power is new;
and because you live in high Heaven,
you think you're beyond the reach of grief.
But I have news for you.
I've already seen two tyrant Fathers—
first Father Sky, then Father Cronus—
overthrown by their sons.
And I assure you,
a third tyrant Father,
our current Lord and God, Zeus,
will also be overthrown by his son.

Do you think I'm afraid to say these things?
Do you think I'm afraid of Zeus?
No, not a bit. So, for all your trouble
of coming here,
you may as well go back where you came from.
For I shall never reveal the names
of the mother and son.

HERMES: Such insolence!
It has brought you to your present state!

PROMETHEUS: It was not Insolence
that bound and tortures me.
It was Zeus!
Even so, I would not exchange my wretched state
for your glorious service!

HERMES: No doubt it's far better
to serve a rock than God!

PROMETHEUS: Speaking of insolence!

HERMES: Prometheus, you seem to be enjoying
your present state.

PROMETHEUS: "Enjoying" it?
May my enemies know such joy—
and that includes you!

HERMES: Are you blaming me for your misery?

PROMETHEUS: I blame all the Gods
who called the good I did "evil,"
and inflicted this torture on me!

HERMES: You are mad!

PROMETHEUS: If hating one's enemies
is madness, then, yes, I am mad.

HERMES: Prometheus, you would be insufferable
if you were free.

PROMETHEUS: (*Savoring the word*) *Free.*
(*Despairing*) Ah, me!

HERMES: "Ah, me!" is a phrase
Zeus does not know.

PROMETHEUS: Not yet, he doesn't.
But as Time grows older,
it teaches everything to everyone.

HERMES: It hasn't taught you common sense!

PROMETHEUS: If it had,
I certainly wouldn't be talking to you!

HERMES: I think you don't intend
to answer Zeus's demands.

PROMETHEUS: Let us say
I am indebted to him for his favors to me,
and I would gladly repay him.
Do you understand?

HERMES: You speak to me as if I were a child!

PROMETHEUS: No. You are simpler than a child
if you were expecting an answer from me.
For no torture device has yet been invented
that can wring anything from me
until my chains are broken and I am set free.

Let Zeus hurl lightning with thunder pealing!
Let him send a blinding snowstorm!
Let him send an earthquake
that sets the whole Earth reeling!
None of these will ever force me
to reveal the name of the woman whose son
will hurl Zeus from his throne.

HERMES: Prometheus, what do you gain
by your attitude?

PROMETHEUS: My "attitude"?
That was determined long ago.

HERMES: You are perverse
and you are a fool!

For God's sake, get some sense!
I think you're not even aware
of how greatly you suffer!

PROMETHEUS: You cannot make me
change my mind
anymore than you can persuade
a wave of the sea
to reverse its direction!
Do you really think I'm so terrified of Zeus
that like a woman I'll lift my face to Heaven,
and pray to the God I hate
to release me from my bondage?
I will never do that!

HERMES: I see I've wasted all my words.
Nothing I've said
has made you change your mind.
You are like an unbroken colt
who fights the bit in his teeth
and kicks against the reins.
But your stubbornness is simply foolishness
for it accomplishes nothing.

Well, since I cannot persuade you,
I have to make you painfully aware
that a terrible storm and a towering wave
will soon break upon you.
There's no escape.
Zeus will strike this jagged cliff

with flaming lightning and thunder,
and will send you—
while the rock still holds you in its embrace—
into the abyss; and you will be buried
under an avalanche of falling rock.

Only the long passage of time
and the working of the elements
will begin to dig you out;
and once again you will see the light of day.
Then, Zeus's black eagle,
ravenously hungry,
will come uninvited to a banquet—
feasting upon your liver—
while with its talons
clawing and gashing your body.
This will continue through the day
until that bird is sated,
and no longer colored black but red,
covered with gore and blood,
and flies off.
During the night your liver will regenerate,
and provide the eagle with the next day's feast.

All I say is true and will be accomplished,
for the mouth of God has spoken it,
and Zeus does not know how to lie.
So give it careful thought,
and never believe out of stubborn pride
that it's better to hold onto a mistaken notion

than to follow good advice.

CHORUS LEADER: Prometheus,
we have to say we agree with Hermes.
It is shameful for the wise to persist in their view
when they know that they are wrong.

PROMETHEUS: The message
that fellow has announced
so loudly every one could hear
is not news to me.
But there's no disgrace
in suffering wrongly
at the hands of one's enemy.

Let the lightning flash and strike!
Let the sky tremble with thunder!
Let the air roar with raging winds!
Let an earthquake shake
and lift the Earth from its foundations!
Let the waves of the sea leap up
and mingle with the stars!
Let Zeus seize my body, lift it on high,
and hurl it into the abyss!
Whatever he does, he cannot kill me,
for I am an immortal God!

HERMES: I hear the ravings of a lunatic.
You are completely mad!
Will your insanity never end?!

Zeus is king of Heaven and Earth,
and intends to remain so.
He is wise, and makes immutable laws,
and they are eternal,
however violent and terrifying
they seem to you.
His are the laws of nature and the universe.
They are not concerned with good and evil,
with right and wrong.

Zeus brings Justice impartially
through laws you do not understand.
You are impertinent
to expect God to show kindness
as you and your beloved Humanity show
kindness,
or to show love
as you and your beloved Humanity show love.
The great God moves in ways
neither ordinary Gods nor man can understand.

Even so, Zeus is not without a Justice.
You can understand
he is punishing you, is he not,
for stealing the Heavenly Fire
that belongs only to the Gods?—
for saving people,
when it was his intention to annihilate them?—
for giving them Blind Hope,
when immortality is not going to be theirs?

And is death really so bad?
Prometheus, isn't it ironic
that you long for death,
when you are doomed never to die?!

(*The reddish-black sky of an impending storm begins to obscure the stars and moon.*)

HERMES: Water Nymphs,
so sympathetic to Prometheus,
listen to me! Leave this place at once!
Save yourselves before the flashes of lightning
and the roar of thunder bewilder your senses!

CHORUS LEADER: Hermes, we are not afraid
to suffer the same fate as Prometheus.
I detest those who desert their friends in adversity.

HERMES: Water Nymphs, if you had the power
to depose Zeus and let Prometheus reign,
do you think that would make a better world?
One day the Humanity that Prometheus loves,
and for whom he suffers so much,
may destroy itself
with the very Fire Prometheus stole for them.
So I ask you, should that occur,
what will Prometheus have accomplished
by giving Humanity the gift of Fire?

Well, Water Nymphs, I have finished.

You are deliberately walking
into the net of disaster.
But never say I didn't warn you.
And do not blame Zeus,
when you've only yourselves to blame.

(HERMES *flies off. Immediately there follows a flash of lightning followed by the rumbling of distant thunder.*)

PROMETHEUS: Water Nymphs,
if you really love me, do what Hermes asks.
Leave this place at once!
I don't want you to suffer
for things I have done. Go!

CHORUS LEADER: (*Looking at the others in puzzlement, not knowing what to do; then decisively*) Goodbye, Prometheus.

CHORUS: (*Together*) Goodbye, Prometheus.

PROMETHEUS: Goodbye, dear friends.

(*The* CHORUS *flies off. Shortly thereafter the storm breaks.*)

PROMETHEUS: It is happening.

(*Rumbling of an earthquake*) The Earth shakes.

(*Flash of lightning*) The lightning flashes.

(*Rumbling of thunder*) The thunder peals
and reverberates.

(*Roaring of the sea*) The sea roars.

(*Howling of the wind*) The wind howls.

(*Flurries of swirling snow and sounds of high winds*)
The whirlwind swirls the snow
in tumultuous conflict
and leaps out from all directions.

(*Great pounding of surf*)
The sky is confounded with the sea.

(*Shouting over the storm*)
It is Zeus who brings this storm
to terrorize and smite me!

O Earth, our mother,
loved by every living creature!
O Sky, our father, watching over everything!
Behold and see the wrongs I suffer
for my love of Humanity!

(*A bolt of lighting strikes the summit. There is a loud cracking sound, followed by a loud clap of thunder. The blizzard makes it impossible to see* PROMETHEUS. *The boulder to which he is bound separates from the summit, and disappears. The blizzard abruptly ends, which brings silence and an empty stage. Darkness descends.*)

THE END

ABOUT THE AUTHOR

Howard Rubenstein is a physician, writer, and photographer. He was born in 1931 in Chicago, where he graduated from Lake View High School. He received a B.A. magna cum laude from Carleton College, where he was elected to Phi Beta Kappa and Sigma Xi and won the Noyes Prize for excellence in ancient Greek. In 1957 Rubenstein received an M.D. from Harvard Medical School. In 1967 he was appointed Physician and Chief of Allergy at the Harvard University Health Services. In 1989 he was appointed a Medical Consultant to the Department of Social Services, state of California. In 2000 he retired from the practice of medicine but has continued to write and take photographs. He is listed in *Who's Who in America* and *Who's Who in the World*.

Prometheus Bound is Rubenstein's third translation or adaptation of an ancient Greek play. The other two are Aeschylus's *Agamemnon* and Euripides' *The Trojan Women*. He has also translated and adapted Jean Racine's *Britannicus*. All these have been produced and published.